Endorsements:

"This story is a very sensitive portrayal of a little dog"
"It had me smiling from the beginning to the end"
"It is well worth reading"

Roberta Hansen

"I highly recommend this book to children (and adult children) of all ages!"
"It was full of humor, sensitivity and fun!"
"An inspiring, delightful story for children and their parents."

Susan Finley
Elementary School teacher and Happiness Life Coach

As a first and second grade reading teacher, my students will love reading this adorable rhyming story!
Great for kids and dog-loving adults as well.

Jennifer Lehman

My young son really enjoyed this book, and loved the rhyming!

Michelle Baker

I0088263

Milo

A Rhyming Autobiography for Your Child

Copyright © 2014 by David Paul Hansen

All rights reserved. No part of this publication may be reproduced, stored in a retrieval system, or transmitted by any means – electronic, mechanical, photographic (photocopying), recording, or otherwise – without prior permission in writing from the author.

Printed in the United States of America
ISBN-13: 978-0692203408 (David Paul Hansen)

www.MilosPage.com
April, 2014

Presented to:

From:

Date:

Table of Contents

**To my wife
Karen Hansen.**

I will never admit it but this book was her idea and without her this story would never have become a reality.

Hello I'm Milo.....

Hi friends, Milo is my name, and I am always ready to play a fun new game.

I am fearless and brave and a very proud dog, but my friend Cricket said I look like a hog.

I don't care what Cricket says, she's jealous of me. She's always running in circles like she's got to go pee.

I have fawn colored fur with a dark black mask; I'm always the pooch that's up for the task.

When I'm on the move my tail curls way up over my butt; that's when it's easy to see I'm sure not no mutt.

I once heard my Dad say my type of breed is a "Pug". I wasn't sure if this was good or bad, but then he said I was cute as a bug!

1

I thought, "oh no" what kind of bug? I was hoping not something like an ugly slug.

When I think back, back when I was a wee little pup, some of these names made my back hairs stand up.

Every hog or bug I have ever seen is just plain ugly, how are these names ever going to make me feel warm and snugly?

Some names that stick, and come to mind fairly quick, would be pig, hog, log, frog…. bug, slug, even ugly mug….Maybe someone hit me with a boxing glove, and having a face only a mother could love!

All these names were hard to take at first; I was called so many names I just wanted to burst.

Now that I am three, I am strong as a tree.

I am very determined in my way; with what I have been through no childish name calling could make me bend, break or sway.

But if you are strong, and want to go on, I'll share my story with you.

Keep in mind my story is not for the faint of heart, but I promise by the end you will see how I tossed away those names and made a bright fresh start.

END CHAPTER

First Memories...

First saw my Mum and remember her well, she is so confident and proud, and I do love her smell.

Three brothers, four sisters, too much yelping going on; I want to sleep so bad with barely the strength to yawn.

No room, no room, someone's always sitting on me; so many brothers, so many sisters, I look up but can't see.

I do love dinner time, I want to get out in front; I feel like a big dog on a big game hunt.

A big flat tray of food and some water to drink, when finished eating we take turns sliding through like an ice skating rink.

I get scared in the night, I don't know why the big fright, I do wish someone would hurry and turn on that night light.

Bedtime is my favorite time of day, to the bottom of the puppy pile is where I want to lay.

So warm and toasty down here I let out a sigh; knowing my mom is standing guard keeping her watchful eye.

With the new day brings play time again, we all jump up and leap out from our warm cuddly den.

Weeks go past and it's been such a blast, but I notice strange people stop by; they look us up and down with a very concerned eye.

I hear my brothers talking so excited they all are; they said these new people may take us home, home in their car.

Wouldn't that be so much fun to have my own girl or boy; so much fun just like a brand new toy!

I love to play hard, I love to rough and tumble, my sister said when more people come by you should simmer down and be humble.

She said no one will pick a pup that's wild like you; no one wants a crazy pup that belongs in a zoo.

The next day we were all playing tag, I'm faster than everyone but I'm not one to brag.

I can easily see that no one can catch me; around a corner so fast, face first into an old woman's knee.

She looked down at me and looked so glum, she said, "I don't want this one; this pup is wild as they come"!

She picked up my sister and headed for the door. My sister hollered back, "take my advice, don't be the last pup on the floor".

I started to worry, I started to get real sad, what if no one wants me; this would be very, very bad.

What if my sister was right, what would I do then? What if it was just me alone in that big dog den?

I must think real hard, as hard as I can; I need to think up a whole brand new plan.

I must try to be more like my sis, the next new person I will act quiet and shy with a soft gentle kiss.

What is that, what can it be? I hear a car outside, let me run to the window and see.

It's a man and woman I have never seen before, I am so nervous cause they are headed right for our front door.

Let me run to the fireplace and lay quietly on the rug, they will surely take me home so I can be their happy little pug.

They both walked in and looked nice as could be; they said "we will take this one", he seems sweet as a pea.

I was so happy I felt like barking aloud, I was so very happy with my head in a cloud.

I wanted to run and bark and tear something apart, but I must be calm and act like a little sweet heart!

"In the back seat Milo", said the man's wife, I am so very happy to start my new life.

END CHAPTER

My new home...

We drove a long time passing so many streets; I wish we would get home because I'm hungry for treats.

We pulled in the driveway and it seemed like a nice place, I bet there will be so much to do with plenty of space.

Into the house just as fast as I could, sliding on every turn cause these floors are all wood.

This is so much fun and these chairs taste so good, my new Mommy is running my way yelling something about shouldn't or should.

I don't know what she said but it's all very funny; she picked me up real fast as I barked, "Wait those chairs taste like honey".

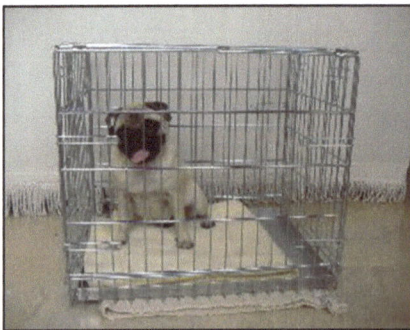

Heading for a cage was the next thing I knew, it all happened so fast I didn't have a clue.

Many weeks went by locked up in this cage, too much time spent in here for a pup of my young age.

These people don't want a pup like me; a pup like my sister is what they really wanted to see.

My sister told me I should settle down, could she have been wrong when she told me to not be a clown?

New people have stopped over just like before; maybe my mom and dad are mad at me for peeing on their floor.

This new man seems to be very curious about me; I will show him what I'm made of if they open this cage and set me free.

This man looks much younger than my mom and dad; maybe he'll play rough and tumble with me without getting mad.

What if I got a new family? What if I got a new home? a dad that let me out of this metal cage so I could rough, tumble and roam.

They opened the cage and I jumped out like a shot, maybe he'll like how fast I am, maybe he'll like it a lot.

I ran around the room and barked at this new man, I said "come down and play and catch me if you can".

He began laughing, maybe thought I was cute; I ran up to him real fast and started biting his boot.

He shook his foot while laughing out loud; on the couch I leaped then turned back to him so proud.

Next thing I knew we were sitting in his car, you better believe I felt just like a star.

At home he put me up on his kitchen table; I was very scared up so high, I hate to admit it but it's really no lie.

My new dad has so many friends, there's always someone new; some are girls, I really like that too.

My sister thought I was a crazy little bee, but look how it ended up, and I was just being me.

END CHAPTER

BIG BIG Trouble...

Back in my dad's car for a visit to his father and mother; he said they have a pup almost my age, would be like a brother.

I thought this should be fun, I could teach the little guy how to really run.

The pup ran out when we got to their place, he was so big I couldn't even look him in the face!

This is no dog, he looks like a horse, and I knew he wanted to eat me as his main course!

They called him Czar, (sounds like ZAR) I was so scared because he was big as a car!

This was a mean dog he could hurt me with just one whack; I knew by his look he was planning his attack.

Dad picked me up, we went to the pool, said we will go for a swim cause it will be real cool.

Dad said "wait one minute I'll go get my bathing suit on"; I thought heck with this, I should run like a fawn.

I don't need a big mean pup that wants to eat me; or a swimming pool with water deep as the sea.

I need to figure a way to somehow break free; waiting for that mean dog to go inside is the key.

Now is my chance to squeeze under the pool gate; he won't see me leaving, that mean dog that I hate.

Heading towards the road silently as a mouse; dad will be surprised when he sees me back home at our house.

This will be easy, not a car in sight, I will run on the sidewalk and be home by late night.

A few cars have stopped and tried to pick me up, but no one can catch me because I'm a quick little pup.

It's starting to get dark and I am all out of smiles, I am getting real scared cause I have been running for miles.

I'm not sure which way to turn already, but I need to stay on track and keep my pace steady.

I'm at an intersection and don't know whether to turn left or right, someone just grabbed me real tight! I need to wiggle around and give them a good bite!

It's a woman and she is taking me in her van, she put me in the back seat right next to a man.

When they stop this van I should jump out like a frog, I should have taken my chances at home with that big mean dog.

I wish I'd stayed home with my dad; I have no idea where they're taking me, and I'm so very sad.

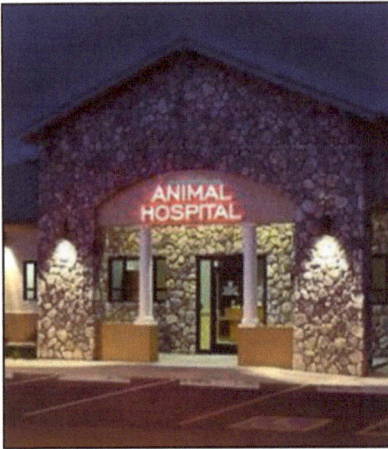

We pulled in somewhere and are slowly parking; I can't break free but I will keep barking.

They held me tight and carried me in; another man was just inside the door with a long white coat and a very happy grin.

This man set down a dish of water I then took a sip; he waved something over my back and said "you're a lucky pup because of your ID chip".

How am I so lucky because I'm back in a cage? I remember always being in here at a very

young age.

He said, "don't worry little guy because your Dad's on his way"; I was so very happy because white coat man just made my day!

I was so very tired I must lay down for awhile; thinking I should have never left, should have never walked that first mile.

Pulling me from this cage still asleep and kind of mad; but I caught a whiff and could tell it was my good ole Dad.

I was so happy to see his face I started to cry, he was happy to see me too, I could tell by the tear in his eye.

Everyone was so excited to see me as we walked in the door, but I was so tired I just passed out on the floor.

When I woke in the morning gaining the strength to crawl; the first thing I saw was

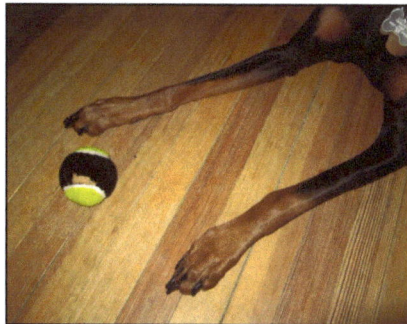

that big bad dog and his tennis ball.

I looked up at him mean and tough; I was hoping he would back off and fall for my bluff.

He lowered his nose and pushed the ball my way; he asked if I wanted to go outside with him and play.

I can't believe what he just said; I was so scared of what I imagined in my head.

Yesterday I was so scared I wanted to run away, today I am so happy I only want to stay.

Czar said "let's be friends" as he turned and yawned; let's first get a drink of water from the ole fish pond.

END CHAPTER

Back Home...

Back at my dad's place I'm always on the run, friends stop over the apartment, it's usually quite fun.

Friends over till late hours of the night, sometimes when they're sleeping I will give them a little bite.

I run and hide laughing so hard, they have no idea what happened because I caught them off guard.

They wake curious wondering if it's real or a dream, I watch from under the chair laughing because they're unaware of my scheme.

I have done this over and over so many times; it's always one of my funniest of crimes.

Dad on the couch with one foot on the floor; I knew he was fast asleep because I could hear his rumbling snore.

I crept up silently as a mouse about to give a quick bite; *dad jumped and screamed* **"MILO"**! This gave me a very scary fright.

So scared I jumped six feet off the floor, running before I landed, heading for the door.

Before I stopped running I heard him laughing so hard; he hollered, "How's it feel now Milo to be the pup caught off guard!"

My game was great fun while it lasted, but it wasn't any fun when I was the one that got blasted.

Next morning I woke to the sound of the bathroom shower, I thought who could possibly be up at this early hour?

I found Dad with wet hair and a comb, he said "I hope you really liked Czar because we're moving back home."

I thought to myself, I will love to play with Czar where I can run outside, there are acres to play rough and tumble because I'm never leashed or tied.

He said we're moving back to the guest house because your Grandma is very sick; I know she will be doing much better once I give her my big puppy lick.

Back home Grandpa walked out with a special collar and a treat, said this collar will keep me from ever going near that very busy street.

I was curious about the collar and walked toward the front street, it started going crazy so I turned full retreat.

Months go by and Czar & I play all day long, I didn't like him at first but I was so very wrong.

Last night a loud truck came and parked on the side; it had big flashy lights, and then they lifted Grandma inside.

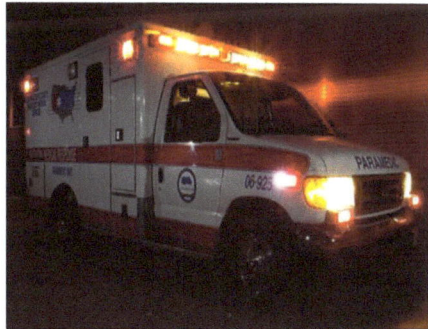

Grandpa and Dad followed close behind, Czar stayed with me because we're two of a kind.

Czar is certainly my best and only friend; we play rough & tumble with endless time to spend.

For a week a man comes to let us out and play; he feeds us a lot more than usual, I do hope he'll stay.

Today we found a rock that could get up and move around, Czar barked at it, but it didn't make a sound!

I pushed on it a few times with my nose; it sucked its head back into its body and then did the same with its toes.

Dad and Grandpa are parking the car; we're running to greet them, me and my best friend Czar.

We all missed each other a lot I could tell by their cries, they gave us the biggest hugs ever with tears in their eyes.

A long time I waited and kept an eye out for that big flashy truck; they never did bring Grandma back, never had such luck.

Grandma always treated me as if I was her best little guy, but all I can do now is take a deep breath and sigh.

Czar told me that he is so very sad; some of his first memories were of Grandma, when he was just a wee little lad.

Lately when Czar and I go outside we don't even play; sometimes we just like to walk especially now that the weather feels gray.

At the ole fish pond is where we will lay away the day; this is where Czar and I first became friends, and first started to play.

Winter has passed and we're enjoying the sun, picking up leaves and sticks and eating them can be such great fun.

I do hope its forever; I hope that's how long Czar and I will be playing together.

END CHAPTER

New Friends...

Grandpa's new friend always kisses the end of my snout; then she hug's me so tight it feels like my eyes will pop out!

So much hugging and kissing I wonder if I should run and hide, Czar said he didn't understand it either, but it does make him warm inside.

Now that I think of it Czar is right; I got warm inside too but thought it was just a bug bite.

She brought over her two dogs, Cricket & Boo-boo just the other day; Czar got in a fight with both, when he should just play.

Czar told me that he didn't like the big one; said "she is ugly and dumb, and not any fun".

I said, "But you didn't give either one a chance; you made your mind up from only the first glance.

I sat Czar down and tried to explain what I had learned; I told him I once made the same mistake but in the end my attitude had turned.

I told him, "there's plenty of time not to like them down the road; but let's start by being nice and kind, at least that's what my experience showed".

Czar told me he would try his best to be kind; he said, "There are so many differences between us, if you don't see that you must be blind".

Besides he said, "What kind of name is Boo-Boo; unless she has on a tutu while stepping in some doo-doo".

"Oh very funny" I replied, but what kind of name is Czar? unless you like to eat tar, while sitting in the back seat of a car?

Grandpa and his dog squeezer friend got our leashes while looking at the clock; he said, "We're taking the time to have a three mile trip around the block"; said, "we will all be a much closer pack after a long-long walk".

The next day I saw Boo-boo and Czar lying in the front lawn like old friends; I did a double take because I thought they looked just like book ends.

Boo-boo is such a prissy girl that hates to get her feet muddy; she's a Doberman just like Czar and now she's his buddy.

Yesterday I saw Boo-boo walk through a puddle by mistake; such a disgusted look, it was a look I will never shake.

But that's ok, Boo-boo is always a good girl to me; Cricket is a nut and she is as crazy as can be.

Way in the back in the wetlands leading to the creek; Cricket will jump off the dock into ice cold water without even a squeak!

She will hop through water that's two feet deep, there could be alligators and snakes just ready to leap!

Hopping up on a cypress tree that's been down for years; looking back at us listening with her cute fuzzy ears.

I heard Grandpa's friend say that Cricket is an Australian Cattle Dog; she tries to rustle up every animal in the wet lands even in thick fog.

Just the other day she chased a possum up a tree; I laughed so hard I accidently went pee.

She is a wild little girl no doubt; tracking down every animal she can find with her keen little snout.

We go every day for a trip down to the wet land; we run and play so hard when we get back we can't even stand.

I did enjoy when it was just me and Czar; but I got to admit, having these new friends I sometimes feel like a star.

Czar asked me, "Where's your Dad? He's never around anymore, not even at the pool"; I told him, "I don't know where he is, but I know it's a place called school".

I told them, "I heard he was going to be a Paramedic so he could drive in a big flashy truck; they can also fix broken people who are down on their luck.

These days we spend most of our time with Grandpa and his new friend; the sad part is the girls will go back to their house and our time comes to an end.

Cricket replied, "I got a secret and I'm not going to tell"; us girls are staying right here with you, all you boy dogs that smell!

She then leaped from the dock yelling back to us, "Catch me if you can; only then will I tell you the secret plan."

We all looked as she pulled herself out of the cold water and crawled up on a log; Boo-boo looked at me and Czar and said; "now that's one crazy dog!"

We all turned and walked away from the crazy nut; halfway down the boardwalk I said, "I'm not getting wet but I would like to know the secret of that little mutt".

By the time we walked to the end of the boardwalk Cricket was standing there dripping wet; we don't know how she got there so fast, almost like she took a jet.

Cricket yelled, "They just got married, so me and Boo-boo are here to stay; all four of us can have so much fun with never ending play."

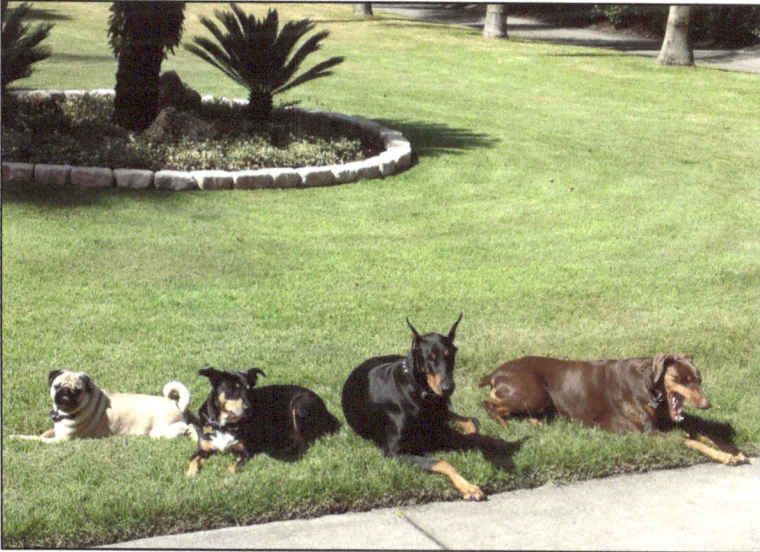

We all looked at each other with so much happiness and joy; it really felt like each of us just got a brand new toy!

END CHAPTER

The Best Things in my life...

Taking time out of my very busy day; thinking of the things I love is the only time that I don't play.

I really like it best when Dad has just cut the lawn; Fresh cut grass smells so fresh it always makes me yawn.

In the front yard laying Froggy style is my best way to lay; back toes curled up under, is the best part of my day.

Some dogs like lying on one side with their back feet tucked up under their nose. I never want to sleep like that, smelling my own stinky toes.

I love the fresh cut grass up under my belly, makes me feel very happy like some warm bread with jelly.

END CHAPTER

What I have learned...

Be true to yourself is what I now see; it doesn't matter what anyone else thinks you should do or be.

As a young pup taking my sister's advice; then I spent time in a cage paying the price.

My sister meant well she did indeed; my first family would have been perfect for her and that's guaranteed.

Never follow the crowd to just fit in; your life will toss and turn in a terrible spin.

When I first met Czar I thought he was a big mean dog that only wanted to hurt me; he looked so big and bad but he is just sweet as a pea.

I ran for miles and miles just to get away from him; now he's the kind of friend for whom I would go out on a limb.

END CHAPTER

Just a little bit more...

Czar said to Boo-boo, "I heard Milo and Grandpa talking; they were saying something about writing a story about Milo, it was quite shocking".

I told all of them that it was true; it's a story of my life and how we all met from my point of view.

Cricket asked if the story of her catching the fish will be in the book; how she pulled it up on shore so we all could take a look.

Boo-boo said, "What about when we found the otter? You got so excited and then fell face first in the water".

I told them, "All of us have so many fun stories we're ready to burst"; but Grandpa said, "what if no one wants to hear about them, we need to know that first".

Cricket said, "Milo, could you ask the kids nicely and say please; after reading this book they write a good review, which would make us happy from our nose to our knees".

What do you say kids, please let us know; just go to the web address that we have below.

www.MilosPage.com

END CHAPTER

ABOUT THE AUTHOR

David Paul Hansen lives in Jacksonville Florida right on the good ole St. Johns River. Almost half of his home's three acres are part of the natural Florida Wetlands, home to all the animals you can imagine. Yes, you will see alligators, snakes and even an occasional Florida Panther, bear and coyote. Once he even saw a monkey which was probably an escapee from a Florida zoo.

Many times throughout his life he has had the opportunity and been encouraged to go hunting, but always thought it would be quite embarrassing bringing home a deer in the back seat of his car on a leash. Always being true animal lovers he and his wife Karen are privileged to be part of a four dog pack.

Living in the middle of this setting, he knows that every day can bring a new exciting adventure. He believes that there may be kids and some adults that just might enjoy these tales.

Contact Information:

Thank you for taking the time to read Milo's Autobiography. I did the best I could helping Milo write this book. As you can imagine he had a somewhat difficult time holding a pen or typing on my keyboard. Through his facial movements and paw gestures, I do believe we were fairly successful in getting everything down on paper.

You can reach Milo at the website www.MilosPage.com.
David Paul Hansen at David@MilosPage.com
www.DavidPaulHansen.com

www.ingramcontent.com/pod-product-compliance
Lightning Source LLC
Chambersburg PA
CBHW040346060426
42445CB00029B/11

* 9 7 8 0 6 9 2 2 0 3 4 0 8 *